Dating Disasters and Other Cosmic Jokes

A Single Girls Guide to the Galaxy

Carl Morton

Chapter 1: Black Hole Exes and Supernova Breakups

When Good Dates Go Bad A Compendium of Disasters

He showed up in Crocs. Not the ironic, hipster kind paired with socks and a knowing grin. No, these were the battle-worn, hole-ridden kind favored by dads mowing the lawn. It was our third date, and up until that point, he'd seemed...normal. We're talking shared love of indie music, witty banter, even a mutual appreciation for obscure documentaries on migratory bird patterns. But those Crocs? They were like a siren, screaming "Run! Flee for the hills while you still can!"

And oh honey, have I run. I've sprinted away from more dating disasters than a track star at the Olympics. There was the guy who spent the entire first date describing his extensive collection of Beanie Babies (mint condition, of course). The one who brought his mom along "for a second opinion." And let's not forget the gentleman who, mid-dinner, decided to floss his teeth with a strand of my hair.

These weren't just bad dates; these were cosmic calamities, proof that the universe has a wicked sense of humor and a penchant for testing my sanity. But through the tears, the awkward silences, and the sheer cringe-worthy moments, I've learned a thing or two about identifying the signs of a disastrous date before it becomes an epic tale of woe worthy of its own Netflix special.

First, trust your gut. That little voice whispering doubts in your ear? It's your intuition, your inner dating guru, and it's rarely wrong. If something feels off, if his charming facade seems a little too rehearsed, if your internal alarm bells are clanging like a fire alarm at a slumber party, pay attention.

Second, watch for red flags, not just waving, but practically doing the Macarena in your face. Is he constantly checking his phone, more interested in Instagram likes than your conversation? Does he interrupt you, talk over you, or worse, spend the entire date regaling you with tales of his ex? Honey, these aren't quirks; they're warning signs, flashing neon arrows pointing you towards the exit.

Third, pay attention to how he treats others. A true gentleman, a keeper, a cosmic catch, will treat everyone with respect, from the waiter to the parking attendant. Watch how he interacts with strangers, how he handles disagreements, how he responds to even the smallest acts of kindness. His true colors will always shine through, especially when he thinks no one is watching.

Now, I know what you're thinking: "But what about the good ones? The ones who slip through the cracks, who seem perfect at first but then morph into dating disasters right before my eyes?"

Ah yes, the wolves in sheep's clothing, the masters of disguise. They're trickier, I'll grant you that, but not impossible to spot. Look for inconsistencies between their words and actions. Does he shower you with compliments but then constantly criticize your choices? Does he promise the world but then fail to follow through on even the simplest of plans? These are red flags disguised as love bombs, and they're just as dangerous.

Remember, dating is a journey, not a destination. It's about exploring, learning, and yes, occasionally encountering a few cosmic jokes along the way. But by trusting your instincts, recognizing red flags, and paying attention to how he treats others, you can navigate the dating universe with confidence, grace, and a healthy dose of humor. And who knows, maybe, just maybe, you'll find yourself sipping cosmic cocktails with a man whose shoe game is as stellar as his personality.

Identifying a Black Hole Ex Gravitys Hold on Your Heart

He lingers. Like the scent of burnt coffee beans, a phantom limb, a melody you can't quite place. He's gone, officially, demonstrably over. You've deleted the texts, burned the photos (metaphorically, of course, fire safety first!), and yet, his gravity still tugs at your heartstrings.

He's the Black Hole Ex, a celestial object so dense, so inescapable, that even light can't escape its pull. You know the type: the one who sucked the joy out of your life, leaving you emotionally drained and questioning your own sanity. He's the master of manipulation, the king of gaslighting, the emperor of emotional unavailability.

The first step to breaking free from his gravitational pull is acknowledging his true nature. This isn't about demonizing him; it's about recognizing the destructive patterns that defined your relationship. Was he emotionally withholding, leaving you constantly craving crumbs of affection? Did he sabotage your happiness, subtly undermining your achievements and dreams? Was he a master of the push-pull, drawing you close only to push you away, leaving you perpetually off-balance?

Remember, you were not the problem. Black Hole Exes thrive on control and manipulation. They seek out partners who are empathetic, compassionate, and eager to please, twisting those beautiful qualities into weapons against you. They'll project their insecurities onto you, blame you for their shortcomings, and convince you that you're lucky to have them, even as they drain the life force from your soul.

So how do you escape the gravitational pull of a Black Hole Ex? It starts with severing all ties. Block his number, unfriend him on social media, and resist the urge to stalk his every online move. Remember, any form of contact, even a seemingly innocent "Happy Birthday" text, is a lifeline he can use to reel you back in.

Next, reclaim your narrative. Black Hole Exes are masters of rewriting history, twisting events to fit their narrative and paint themselves as the victim. Don't buy into it. Journal your experiences, talk to trusted friends and family, and remind yourself of the truth: You deserve to be loved, respected, and cherished, not manipulated, controlled, or emotionally abused.

This is also the time to rebuild your self-esteem. Black Hole Exes are experts at chipping away at your confidence, leaving you feeling unworthy and unlovable. Challenge those negative thoughts. Embrace your strengths, celebrate your accomplishments, and surround yourself with people who lift you up and remind you of your worth.

Healing from a Black Hole Ex is a process, not a race. There will be good days and bad days, moments of strength and waves of grief. Be patient with yourself. Allow yourself to feel the pain, the anger, the confusion, but don't let those emotions define you.

Remember, you are a magnificent being, capable of love, joy, and extraordinary resilience. You escaped the gravitational pull of a Black Hole Ex, and that, my dear, is a testament to your strength. Now go forth and shine your light, brighter and bolder than ever before.

The Art of the Post Date Irish Exit and Other Survival Tactics

Picture this: You're twenty minutes into a blind date, and it's like watching paint dry, only less stimulating. The conversation is drier than a mouthful of saltines, his jokes land flatter than a pancake on the moon, and you're pretty sure you just saw a tumbleweed roll through your peripheral vision. What do you do?

You, my friend, need to master the art of the graceful escape, the strategic retreat, the ever-so-elegant Irish Exit.

Now, before we delve into the delicate art of disappearing, let's be clear: ghosting is never cool. But there's a universe of difference between disappearing mid-date without a word and recognizing when a situation calls for a swift and decisive exit strategy.

The key to a successful Irish Exit is preparation. Before you even set foot out the door, have your escape route mapped out. Tell a friend to call you an hour into the date with a "family emergency" (desperate times, desperate measures). If you're feeling extra cautious, plant a fake voicemail on your phone beforehand, complete with dramatic sniffles and pleas for your immediate return.

Once you've laid the groundwork, it's all about observation and execution. Watch for the signs of a sinking ship: excessive yawning, furtive glances at the door, a conversation that's about as stimulating as watching grass grow. When you feel the urge to fake a sudden illness, it's go time.

Excuse yourself politely, but firmly. "Excuse me a moment, I need to use the restroom" is a classic for a reason. Once you're out of sight, make like a tree and get out of there. No lingering glances, no wistful sighs, just a clean break.

Of course, the Irish Exit is just one tool in your dating survival kit. Here are a few more tips to navigate the treacherous terrain of bad dates:

The Conversation Deflector: He's droning on about his stamp collection again. Time to deploy the conversation deflector. Subtly steer the conversation towards a topic you're genuinely interested in. Who knows, you might even learn something new (or at least avoid slipping into a boredom-induced coma).

The Emergency Escape Pod: This one requires a little pre-planning. Designate a trusted friend as your Emergency Escape Pod. Give them a code word or phrase that, when uttered, signals them to call you immediately with a convincing (and preferably embarrassing) reason to leave.

The Honesty Gambit: Sometimes, the most disarming weapon in your arsenal is honesty. If you're truly miserable, it's okay to politely tell your date that you're not feeling a connection and would like to end the date early. It might sting a little, but it's better than enduring another hour of awkward silence and forced smiles.

Remember, dating is a numbers game. Not every date will be a cosmic connection, and that's okay. The key is to protect your heart, your sanity, and your precious time. So go forth, armed with your wit, your charm, and your trusty survival tactics, and conquer the dating universe one awkward encounter at a time.

From Supernova to Stardust Embracing the Beauty of Breakups

A breakup is a supernova. A cosmic explosion of emotions, shattering your world into a million glittering pieces. There's shock, disbelief, a searing pain that threatens to consume you whole. You might feel like you're freefalling through space, untethered and utterly alone.

It's okay to grieve. Let the tears flow, scream into your pillow, wallow in the unfairness of it all. Surround yourself with your tribe—the friends who bring you comfort food and tissues, who listen without judgment and remind you of your own dazzling brilliance.

But amidst the wreckage, a curious thing happens. As the initial shockwaves subside, you begin to see the beauty in the debris. Those shattered pieces? They're not just fragments of a love lost; they're fragments of you, waiting to be reclaimed, reassembled, and reborn.

This is your opportunity to rediscover yourself, to reconnect with the passions and dreams that might have been dimmed during the relationship. Remember that pottery class you always wanted to take? That solo trip to Tuscany you dreamt of? Now is the time, my friend. Embrace your newfound freedom, explore uncharted territories, and rediscover the joy of doing things that set your soul on fire.

This is also a time for radical self-care. Treat yourself with the same love and tenderness you'd shower on your best friend going through a breakup. Indulge in long baths, nourish your body with healthy food, and prioritize sleep like it's your new religion. Move your body—dance, run, hike—anything that gets your blood pumping and endorphins flowing.

As you heal, you'll start to notice a shift. The pain will lose its sharp edges, the memories will soften, and you'll find yourself smiling again, genuinely smiling, at the simple things: a breathtaking sunset, a perfectly brewed cup of coffee, the sound of your own laughter echoing through your apartment.

This is not to say that you'll erase him from your memory. Some love stories leave an imprint on our hearts, a bittersweet ache that lingers long after the final chapter has been written. But you'll learn to hold those memories with a gentle grace, acknowledging the lessons learned and the growth you've experienced.

For in the ashes of every supernova, new stars are born. And you, my darling, are stardust. You are resilient, radiant, and capable of love more profound than you can possibly imagine. Embrace the beauty of this transformation. Allow yourself to grieve, to heal, to rediscover your own magnificence.

This is your time to shine. Let your light illuminate the universe.

Rebuilding Your Galaxy A Guide to Post Breakup Self Care

The spaceship of your heart has crash-landed. Maybe it was a slow descent, a sputtering engine, a gradual loss of altitude. Or perhaps it was a full-on, fiery explosion, leaving a trail of smoke and debris in its wake. Regardless of how it happened, you're left standing amidst the wreckage, bruised, battered, and wondering how to possibly move forward.

This, my friend, is where the real journey begins. The journey of rebuilding your galaxy, piece by shimmering piece. It's about more than just picking up the pieces; it's about creating something even more beautiful, more resilient, more aligned with the celestial being you truly are.

First, understand this: healing is not linear. There will be days when you're a supernova of strength and resilience, and days when you're a black hole of despair, barely able to get out of bed. Forgive yourself on the dark days, and celebrate your progress on the bright ones. Remember, you're navigating uncharted territory, and there's no right or wrong way to heal.

Now, let's talk practical magic. Self-care isn't just bubble baths and face masks (though those are certainly encouraged!). It's about consciously choosing to nourish your mind, body, and spirit in ways that feel authentic and life-giving.

Start with the foundation: your physical well-being. Fuel your body with nourishing foods that make you feel vibrant and energized. Move your body in ways that bring you joy, whether it's dancing like nobody's watching, finding solace in a yoga flow, or conquering a challenging hike. Prioritize sleep like it's the elixir of life, for it's in the realm of dreams that your heart finds the space to process and heal.

Next, tend to your emotional landscape. Give yourself permission to feel it all—the sadness, the anger, the confusion. Journal your feelings, express yourself through art, or talk to a trusted friend or therapist. Remember, acknowledging your emotions is not a sign of weakness; it's a testament to your strength and capacity for healing.

Your mind, that magnificent, complex universe, needs nurturing too. Challenge negative thought patterns with affirmations that remind you of your worthiness and resilience. Engage in activities that spark your intellect and curiosity—read books that ignite your imagination, lose yourself in thought-provoking podcasts, or delve into a new subject that sets your soul on fire.

Reconnecting with your social galaxy is crucial. Surround yourself with people who lift you higher, who remind you of your brilliance, and who shower you with unconditional love and support. These are your cosmic companions, the ones who'll help you navigate the asteroid fields of heartache and celebrate your victories along the way.

As you rebuild, remember that self-care isn't selfish; it's an act of radical self-love. It's about honoring the sacred vessel of your being and treating yourself with the same kindness and compassion you'd extend to your dearest friend.

This journey won't be easy, but I promise you this: it will be worth it. For in the process of rebuilding your galaxy, you'll discover a strength you never knew you possessed, a resilience that will guide you through any storm, and a capacity for love that knows no bounds.

Chapter 2: Navigating the Asteroid Belt of Online Dating

Creating a Stellar Profile Pictures Bios and Avoiding Catfishing

Your online dating profile is your cosmic billboard, a beacon in the vast digital universe, signaling to potential partners that you've arrived, ready to mingle amongst the stars. But in a sea of faces and carefully curated bios, how do you stand out from the crowd? More importantly, how do you present an authentic version of yourself while dodging the pitfalls of misleading profiles and outright catfishing?

First impressions matter, and nothing makes a stronger impact than your profile picture. This is your cosmic close-up, your chance to showcase your personality and allure. Choose photos that are recent, high-quality, and reflect your true self. A genuine smile is worth a thousand perfectly posed selfies, and a picture of you engaged in a favorite hobby speaks volumes about your passions. Avoid heavily filtered photos or images where you're barely recognizable. Remember, authenticity is attractive!

Now, let's talk about your bio, the cosmic caption that accompanies your stellar image. This is your opportunity to give potential matches a glimpse into your world – your passions, your quirks, your unique brand of stardust. Keep it concise, engaging, and a reflection of your true self. What are you passionate about? What makes you laugh until you cry? What are you looking for in a partner? Be specific, be genuine, and don't be afraid to inject a little humor.

Honesty is the best policy when it comes to your bio. Don't exaggerate your height, accomplishments, or interests to fit in or impress others. Remember, you're looking for someone who appreciates you for you, not a fictionalized version of yourself.

Now, let's navigate the treacherous black holes of catfishing. Sadly, not everyone in the online dating universe is playing by the rules. Some people create fake profiles, using stolen photos and fabricated bios to deceive others.

So how can you protect yourself from these cosmic con artists? First and foremost, trust your instincts. If something feels off – maybe their photos are too perfect, their stories seem too good to be true, or they're reluctant to video chat – trust your gut and proceed with caution.

Be wary of profiles with limited information or photos that all look professionally taken. Pay attention to inconsistencies in their stories or if they seem evasive when you ask specific questions. Reverse image search their photos using Google or TinEye to see if they're being used elsewhere online.

Don't be afraid to ask direct questions about their life, interests, and intentions. A genuine person will be happy to share details about themselves, while a catfish will likely become evasive or defensive.

Finally, remember that you have the power to control your online dating experience. Choose dating apps and websites known for their safety measures and community guidelines. Report any suspicious profiles or behavior to the platform's administrators.

Creating a stellar online dating profile is about striking a balance between presenting your best self and staying true to who you are. By embracing authenticity, being mindful of your digital footprint, and prioritizing safety, you can navigate the online dating universe with confidence and enjoy the exciting journey of connecting with other cosmic souls.

Decoding the Signals What His Messages Really Mean

He's sent you a message. A simple string of words, yet it sets your heart racing, your mind spinning, trying to decipher the hidden meaning behind every emoji and punctuation mark. Welcome to the fascinating, and sometimes frustrating, world of deciphering male communication in the digital age.

Let's be honest, men and women often approach communication from different galaxies. While you might craft carefully worded novels disguised as text messages, he might reply with a succinct "Cool" or a single thumbs-up emoji. But before you assume he's not interested or doesn't care, remember that brevity doesn't always equal disinterest. Men, in all their Martian glory, often communicate in a more direct, less emotionally expressive way.

That being said, there are subtle signals and patterns in his messages that can offer valuable insights into his level of interest and intentions.

First, consider the frequency and timing of his messages. Does he respond promptly, or does he leave you hanging for days on end? While everyone has different communication styles and schedules, consistent effort is a positive sign. If he's making time to message you regularly, even if it's just a quick "Good morning" or to share a funny meme, it suggests he's thinking about you and enjoys your virtual company.

Next, pay attention to the content of his messages. Are they superficial and generic, or does he ask questions, share details about his life, and seem genuinely interested in getting to know you? Does he engage with your stories and reciprocate with anecdotes of his own? When a man is invested, he'll go beyond the superficial and make an effort to connect on a deeper level.

The tone and language he uses can also reveal a lot about his intentions. Does he compliment you genuinely, or are his compliments bordering on cheesy pickup lines? Does he tease you playfully, or are his jokes disrespectful or demeaning? Pay attention to how his words make you feel. Your intuition is a powerful tool, and if something feels off, it probably is.

Emojis, those tiny pictograms that have become an integral part of digital communication, can also offer subtle clues. While their meaning can be subjective, a well-placed heart emoji, a playful wink, or a string of laughing emojis after your joke can indicate warmth, affection, and a desire to flirt. However, don't read too much into a single emoji. Context is key, and it's always best to look for patterns in his communication style rather than overanalyzing individual messages.

Finally, remember that the most direct way to know what he means is to simply ask. Don't be afraid to communicate your needs and expectations clearly and directly. If his vague responses or inconsistent communication style are leaving you feeling confused or insecure, address it openly and honestly. Healthy communication is the foundation of any strong relationship, and that includes being able to express your needs and expectations without fear of judgment or rejection.

Decoding male communication can feel like learning a new language, but by paying attention to the subtle signals, trusting your instincts, and communicating openly and honestly, you can navigate the digital dating landscape with confidence and clarity.

Swiping Right on Safety Navigating the Online Dating Universe with Confidence

The world of online dating, with its endless possibilities and promise of connection at your fingertips, can be exhilarating. It's a digital dance floor where you can connect with people who share your interests, values, and desire for companionship. However, just as you wouldn't walk into a crowded bar without taking precautions, it's crucial to approach online dating with a healthy dose of caution and prioritize your safety.

Think of your online dating journey as embarking on a trek through an exciting but unfamiliar galaxy. You'll encounter breathtaking nebulas of potential, but it's also wise to be aware of the occasional black hole.

Your first line of defense is information. Choose your dating apps wisely. Research different platforms and opt for those known for their safety measures, active moderation, and robust privacy settings. Some platforms offer features like photo verification, which can help weed out fake profiles and increase your chances of connecting with genuine individuals.

Before diving headfirst into the cosmic pool of potential matches, take your time crafting a profile that reflects your true self while safeguarding your privacy. Avoid sharing personal details like your home address, workplace, or any information that could be used to locate you in the real world.

When it comes to choosing your profile pictures, opt for images that showcase your personality and interests without revealing sensitive locations. A photo of you enjoying your favorite hiking trail is great, but make sure it's not easily identifiable as your go-to spot.

Communication is key in any relationship, and online dating is no exception. Initially, keep your conversations within the app's messaging system. This allows the platform to monitor for inappropriate behavior and provides an extra layer of security. As you get to know someone better and feel more comfortable, you can suggest moving the conversation to a phone call or video chat.

Speaking of video chats, consider them your cosmic screening tool. A video call allows you to verify the person is who they claim to be in their profile and can provide valuable insights into their demeanor and communication style. Plus, it's a fun way to gauge your chemistry before meeting in person.

When the time comes to meet offline, don't throw caution to the solar winds. Arrange the first few dates in public places, and let a trusted friend or family member know your plans, including your date's name and the location of the meeting. Offer to share your location with them during the date for an extra layer of security.

Trust your instincts. If something feels off – maybe their stories seem inconsistent, they're overly eager to meet offline before getting to know you properly, or their communication raises red flags – don't hesitate to end the conversation or block them from contacting you further. Your safety and well-being are paramount, and it's always better to err on the side of caution.

Finally, remember that you're not alone in navigating the online dating universe. If you encounter inappropriate behavior, harassment, or suspect someone is catfishing, don't hesitate to report it to the dating app or website. Most platforms have dedicated teams to investigate and address such issues, and your actions can help protect others from potentially harmful encounters.

Online dating can be a wonderful way to meet new people and explore potential romantic connections. By prioritizing your safety and following these tips, you can confidently navigate the digital dating cosmos and enjoy the journey of finding your own personal supernova.

Chapter 3: First Contact Mastering the Art of the First Few Dates

Location Location Location Choosing the Perfect First Date Spot

Location, location, location. It's the age-old mantra for real estate, but it holds surprisingly true for first dates too. Think about it: a first date is about making a good impression, creating a comfortable atmosphere, and, most importantly, getting to know someone. The 'where' of it all plays a surprisingly significant role in setting the stage for all of that.

Choosing the wrong location can lead to awkward silences, forced conversation, and a swift end to any potential romance. Remember that bustling pub you love with your friends? The one with the live band and the raucous laughter? Amazing for a Friday night out, a death knell for a first date. The key is to find a place that encourages conversation and connection, not one that actively fights against it.

So, where to begin? Start by ditching the tired dinner-and-a-movie formula. It's predictable, it lacks originality, and frankly, it puts undue pressure on both parties. Instead, think about the things you enjoy, the places that make you feel comfortable, and most importantly, the activities that allow for natural conversation.

Coffee shops are a classic for a reason. They offer a casual, low-pressure environment to chat, and the caffeine boost doesn't hurt either. Look for a place with a cozy atmosphere, perhaps one with comfortable armchairs or a sunny patio. Bonus points for interesting decor or a unique menu that can spark conversation.

If you're both active individuals, consider incorporating some movement into your date. A walk or bike ride through a scenic park, a visit to a botanical garden, or even a fun game of mini-golf can provide ample opportunity for conversation and laughter. These activities also take the pressure off maintaining constant eye contact, which can be a relief for some.

For the culturally inclined, museums, art galleries, and historical sites offer endless conversation starters. Discussing your favorite exhibits or sharing your knowledge can reveal shared interests and provide glimpses into each other's perspectives.

Don't underestimate the power of a shared experience, even a simple one. Visiting a local farmer's market, trying out a new cooking class, or attending a book reading can create lasting memories and provide plenty of talking points.

Above all, be mindful of your date's interests and comfort levels. If you're unsure about their preferences, don't be afraid to suggest a few options and choose together. It shows that you're considerate and invested in creating a positive experience for both of you.

The most important thing to remember is that the location is simply a backdrop for the real focus: getting to know each other. Choose a place that feels authentic to you, encourages conversation, and sets the stage for a relaxed and enjoyable experience. After all, the best first date spot is one that allows your personalities and connection to shine through.

Conversation Constellations Sparkling Conversation Starters and Avoiding Awkward Silences

The first date jitters. We've all been there – the nervous anticipation, the butterflies in your stomach, and that nagging fear of awkward silences stretching on like an eternity. But what if I told you that conversation, even on a first date, doesn't have to be a minefield of potential awkwardness? What if it could be a journey of discovery, a shared exploration of thoughts, dreams, and passions?

Think of a conversation as a constellation. Each person's thoughts and experiences are like individual stars, scattered across the vast expanse of the universe. Your job is to connect those stars, to find the threads that weave them together into a beautiful, sparkling whole.

So, how do you do it? How do you become a conversational astronomer, guiding the dialogue and uncovering those hidden gems of connection? It starts with ditching the tired, generic questions. "What do you do?" and "Where are you from?" are conversation killers, leading to dead-end answers and missed opportunities for genuine connection.

Instead, aim for open-ended questions that invite your date to share their stories, passions, and perspectives. Ask about their favorite travel memory, the book that's stayed with them long after they've finished it, or the hobby they could lose themselves in for hours. These questions spark the imagination and encourage your date to reveal more of themselves.

But it's not just about asking the right questions; it's about being an active and engaged listener. Put away your phone, silence those mental to-do lists, and truly focus on what your date is saying. Listen not just to their words, but to the emotions and experiences they convey. Ask follow-up questions, share your own related anecdotes, and show genuine interest in their world.

Remember those shared experiences we talked about earlier? This is where they really come into play. Did you both grow up watching the same TV show? Did a particular song or band resonate with both of you? Shared cultural touchstones are like conversational gold, providing a springboard for reminiscing, laughter, and instant connection.

Don't be afraid to inject a little humor into the conversation. Sharing a funny observation, a lighthearted anecdote, or even a well-timed self-deprecating joke can break the ice, ease any tension, and create a more relaxed and enjoyable atmosphere.

If, despite your best efforts, a lull in the conversation does occur, don't panic. It's perfectly natural for conversations to ebb and flow. Use these moments as opportunities to observe your surroundings, comment on the ambiance of the location you chose (remember, location, location, location!), or simply take a breath and re-engage when you're ready.

Remember, a first date is not an interrogation. It's about finding common ground, sparking curiosity, and leaving the other person wanting more. So relax, be yourself, and let the conversation unfold organically. You might be surprised at the connections you make and the stories you uncover when you approach conversation as an exploration, a journey of shared discovery.

And if, by chance, the conversation does hit a dead end? Well, at least you've had a chance to practice your conversational astronomy. Every interaction, whether it leads to a second date or not, is an opportunity to refine your skills and become a master conversationalist, ready to navigate the cosmos of human connection.

Reading Between the Lines Body Language and Other Subtle Signals

We communicate in a symphony of unspoken cues. Our words, carefully chosen as they may be, are only a fraction of the story we tell. Our bodies, with their subtle shifts and gestures, are constantly broadcasting a parallel narrative, a language of leans, glances, and unconscious movements. Learning to decipher this language, especially in the delicate ecosystem of a first date, can be the key to unlocking a deeper understanding of your companion.

Let's start with the basics: eye contact. Those windows to the soul, as they say, speak volumes. A gaze that lingers a beat too long, a playful glance across the table, even the shy aversion of eyes can reveal a world of emotions, from attraction and interest to nervousness and discomfort. Pay attention to how your date uses eye contact. Do they hold your gaze steadily, conveying attentiveness and genuine interest? Or do their eyes dart around the room, betraying boredom or a desire to escape the conversation?

Next, observe their posture. Are they leaning towards you, their body language signaling openness and engagement? Or are they sitting back, arms crossed, creating a physical barrier that speaks of discomfort or disinterest? Mirroring your date's posture, subtly and naturally, can foster a sense of connection and rapport.

Hands, those expressive instruments of gesture, can be particularly revealing. Playing with a napkin, twirling a strand of hair, or fidgeting with a phone can be signs of nervousness, boredom, or even a lack of genuine interest. On the other hand, open gestures, like using hands while speaking or placing a hand gently on your arm during a moment of shared laughter, often signal warmth, connection, and a desire to bridge the physical space between you.

Don't forget about the power of a smile. A genuine smile, one that reaches the eyes and crinkles the corners, is a universal sign of warmth, approachability, and, yes, attraction. It's a non-verbal beacon signaling that you're enjoying the company and the conversation.

Remember, however, that body language is not an exact science. Cultural backgrounds, personal experiences, and individual quirks can influence how people express themselves nonverbally. The key is to look for clusters of cues, patterns of behavior that, taken together, paint a clearer picture of your date's true feelings.

Beyond the physical, pay attention to the nuances of their voice. Does their tone soften when they talk about something they're passionate about? Do they unconsciously mirror your pace and volume, a subtle sign of building rapport? These vocal cues, often overlooked, can provide valuable insights into their emotional state and level of engagement.

Reading between the lines, deciphering the subtle signals woven through body language and vocal tone, is not about uncovering some hidden truth or exposing your date's deepest secrets. It's about developing a deeper understanding of the unspoken language they're speaking, the language of connection, attraction, and shared humanity. It's about becoming fluent in the silent conversation that unfolds beneath the surface, adding layers of meaning and nuance to your interactions.

So, the next time you find yourself on a first date, remember to tune in not just to the words being spoken, but to the symphony of unspoken cues playing out before you. You might be surprised at what you discover.

Chapter 4: Alien Encounters When Your Dating Pool Feels Out of This World

The Case of the Vanishing Act Dealing with Ghosting and Other Elusive Behaviours

Ghosting. It's the dating equivalent of being stuck in a horror movie, a chilling silence descending after what seemed like a promising start. One minute you're exchanging witty banter, making plans for the future, the next – poof! – they've vanished into the ether, leaving you staring at a blank screen and a head full of unanswered questions.

It's a frustrating, often hurtful experience, leaving you questioning your worth and wondering what you could have done differently. But here's the truth: ghosting says more about the ghoster than it does about you. It's a sign of their emotional immaturity, their inability to communicate effectively, and their lack of respect for your time and feelings.

So, how do you deal with the ghost in the machine, the vanishing act that leaves you feeling confused and disheartened? First and foremost, don't blame yourself. It's easy to spiral into self-doubt, to analyze every text message and interaction for clues to what went wrong. But the truth is, you can't control someone else's actions, only your reactions to them.

Recognize that ghosting is a cowardly way to end a potential connection. It's the digital equivalent of running away from a difficult conversation, leaving the other person to pick up the pieces. Remember, you deserve closure, but you're unlikely to find it from someone who resorts to such immature tactics.

If you've been ghosted, allow yourself to feel the disappointment, the hurt, even the anger. It's natural to experience a range of emotions when someone you've invested time and energy in suddenly disappears. But don't let those emotions consume you. Acknowledge them, process them, and then, most importantly, let them go.

Resist the urge to chase after the ghost. Sending a barrage of unanswered texts or pleading for an explanation will only prolong the agony and further diminish your self-worth. Remember, silence speaks volumes. Their inability to respond is all the answer you need.

Instead of dwelling on the what-ifs and why-me's, shift your focus to the incredible person you are. Remind yourself of your strengths, your accomplishments, and the qualities that make you uniquely you. Spend time with people who value and appreciate you, people who wouldn't dream of leaving you hanging.

If the ghoster does resurface, offering a flimsy excuse or a half-hearted apology, remember that you have the power to choose how you engage. You don't owe them your time or attention, especially if they haven't offered a sincere explanation for their disappearance.

The world of dating can be a tricky terrain to navigate, filled with twists, turns, and unexpected detours. Encountering a ghost along the way is never pleasant, but it's important to remember that it's just one small bump in the road. Don't let it derail your journey or diminish your belief in finding genuine connection.

Learn from the experience, dust yourself off, and keep moving forward with your head held high. The right person will not only see your worth, but will cherish the opportunity to get to know you, ghosts and all.

Red Flags from Outer Space Recognizing and Avoiding Toxic Relationship Patterns

Love, as the saying goes, can sometimes feel like a battlefield. But in the heady rush of early romance, it's easy to overlook the red flags waving frantically on the sidelines. We've all been there, blinded by the allure of a new relationship, our judgment clouded by a potent cocktail of hormones and hope. But recognizing and, more importantly, heeding those early warning signs can save you a world of heartache down the line.

One of the most glaring red flags is a lack of respect. Respect forms the bedrock of any healthy relationship, romantic or otherwise. It's about valuing your partner's thoughts, feelings, and boundaries, even when they differ from your own. Disrespect can manifest in subtle ways, like constantly interrupting or dismissing your opinions, or in more overt actions, such as belittling you in front of others or making decisions that impact you without your input.

Control issues are another major red flag, often disguised as "caring" or "protective" behavior. Does your partner constantly question your whereabouts, monitor your social media activity, or try to isolate you from your friends and family? These controlling tendencies can escalate over time, eroding your sense of self and autonomy.

Jealousy, that green-eyed monster, can rear its ugly head in seemingly innocuous ways. While a twinge of jealousy now and then is normal, constant suspicion, accusations, and attempts to restrict your interactions with others are signs of insecurity and a lack of trust, both of which are toxic to a healthy relationship.

Communication is key in any relationship, but it's especially crucial when navigating disagreements and challenges. A partner who shuts down during arguments, resorts to personal attacks, or refuses to take responsibility for their actions is waving a red flag the size of Texas. Healthy communication involves active listening, empathy, and a willingness to find mutually agreeable solutions.

Pay attention to how your partner treats others, especially those they perceive as being in a less powerful position. Do they treat service workers with disdain, speak condescendingly to their family members, or lash out at others when they're feeling stressed? How someone treats those around them is a telling indicator of their true character.

Another red flag to watch out for is a lack of accountability. Everyone makes mistakes in relationships, but a partner who consistently blames others, refuses to acknowledge their shortcomings, or deflects responsibility is unlikely to foster a healthy or fulfilling partnership.

It's important to remember that red flags are not always blatant or easy to spot. They can creep in slowly, disguised as charming quirks or endearing flaws. Trust your instincts. If something feels off, if your gut is screaming at you to proceed with caution, don't ignore it.

Talking about your concerns with a trusted friend, family member, or therapist can provide valuable perspective and support. They can help you see the situation more clearly, identify patterns of toxic behavior, and empower you to make choices that prioritize your well-being.

Remember, you deserve to be in a relationship where you feel respected, valued, and safe. Don't settle for anything less, no matter how dazzling the initial spark. Love shouldn't feel like a battlefield. It should feel like a safe haven, a place where you can be your authentic self, red flags and all.

Embracing Your Inner Weirdo Finding Someone Who Celebrates Your Unique Orbit

We're all a little weird. We have our quirks, our passions, our unique ways of seeing the world. These idiosyncrasies, the things that make us different, are often the very things that make us lovable, interesting, and vibrantly alive. But in the world of dating, where first impressions reign supreme and the pressure to conform can feel overwhelming, it's easy to let those quirks recede into the shadows, to present a polished, generic version of ourselves in the hopes of finding someone who will accept us.

But here's the secret: trying to hide your true self is like trying to fit a square peg into a round hole. It's uncomfortable, unsustainable, and ultimately, unrewarding. True connection, the kind that lights up your soul and makes you feel truly seen, can only blossom when you embrace your inner weirdo, when you let your freak flag fly with unapologetic pride.

Think about it: wouldn't you rather be with someone who celebrates your love of vintage taxidermy, your uncanny ability to quote obscure movie lines, or your passion for competitive air guitar, than someone who barely bats an eyelid? Authenticity is magnetic. When you embrace your true self, quirks and all, you radiate a confidence and magnetism that draws people in, people who appreciate you for the wonderfully weird individual you are.

Finding someone who celebrates your unique orbit starts with celebrating yourself. Embrace the things that make you different, the things that make you laugh, the things that light you up from the inside out. Don't be afraid to share your passions, your quirks, your unique perspective on the world. The right person will not only accept them, but will cherish them as the very things that make you, you.

Look for someone who is also comfortable embracing their own weirdness. Pay attention to how they talk about their passions, their interests, the things that make them tick. Do their eyes light up when they talk about their collection of antique teacups or their encyclopedic knowledge of 80s hair metal bands? Do they embrace the things that make them different, or do they downplay them, afraid to stand out from the crowd?

Shared weirdness is a powerful foundation for a strong and lasting connection. When you find someone who gets your brand of humor, who embraces your quirks, who encourages you to let your freak flag fly, you've found something truly special. You've found someone who sees you, accepts you, and celebrates you for the wonderfully weird individual you are.

Don't be afraid to let your guard down, to be vulnerable, to let your true self shine through. The right person won't just tolerate your quirks, they'll adore them. They'll be your biggest cheerleader, your partner in crime, your fellow traveler on the gloriously weird and wonderful journey of life.

So, go forth and embrace your inner weirdo. The world is waiting to be dazzled by your unique brand of brilliance. And who knows, you might just find someone who thinks your brand of weird is the most amazing thing they've ever seen.

Chapter 5: Relationship Wormholes: Exploring the Mysteries of Love and Commitment

Defining the Relationship: DTR Conversations and Navigating the Commitment Nebula

The early stages of dating can feel like navigating through a beautiful, yet hazy, nebula. There's excitement, intrigue, and a sense of wonder as you get to know someone new. But as the initial sparkle starts to settle, a new kind of question emerges, one that can leave you feeling like you're stumbling through a cosmic cloud of uncertainty: "What are we?"

Defining the relationship, often referred to as the "DTR" conversation, can be a daunting prospect. It involves vulnerability, the risk of rejection, and the potential to disrupt the comfortable ambiguity that often defines the early stages of dating. However, it's a crucial step in moving from a place of uncertainty to one of clarity, understanding, and shared expectations.

The timing of the DTR conversation is unique to each relationship. There's no magic formula or set timeframe. Some couples naturally fall into a defined relationship after a few dates, while others take weeks or even months to have the "what are we?" talk. The key is to initiate the conversation when you feel a shift in your own expectations and desires.

Before you launch into the DTR conversation, it's important to take stock of your own feelings and expectations. What are you hoping to gain from defining the relationship? Are you looking for exclusivity, a commitment to a future together, or simply a better understanding of where you stand?

Once you have a clear sense of your own needs and desires, it's time to have an open and honest conversation with your partner. Choose a time and place where you both feel comfortable and can talk freely without distractions. Approach the conversation with a spirit of curiosity and respect, remembering that the goal is to understand each other's perspectives, not to pressure your partner into a commitment they're not ready for.

Start by expressing your feelings and what you're looking for in a relationship. Use "I" statements to avoid placing blame or making your partner feel defensive. For example, instead of saying, "You never call me back," try something like, "I feel a little insecure when I don't hear from you for a few days."

Listen attentively to your partner's response, seeking to understand their perspective and what they're looking for in a relationship. Remember, communication is a two-way street. It's not just about expressing your own needs and desires, but also about actively listening to and respecting your partner's.

If your expectations for the relationship align, congratulations! You've successfully navigated the commitment nebula and emerged with a shared understanding of where you stand. Celebrate this milestone and enjoy the journey of getting to know each other on a deeper level.

However, if your expectations don't align, it's important to acknowledge and respect those differences. It's possible that one of you is looking for a serious commitment while the other is content with a more casual arrangement. In these situations, honesty and open communication are crucial. It's better to acknowledge the incompatibility early on than to continue investing in a relationship that ultimately won't meet your needs.

Defining the relationship can be a nerve-wracking experience, but it's a necessary step in moving from a place of uncertainty to one of clarity and shared understanding. By approaching the conversation with honesty, respect, and a willingness to listen, you can navigate the commitment nebula with grace and emerge with a stronger, more fulfilling connection.

Introducing Your Partner to Your Universe Family Friends and the Art of Interstellar Integration

Meeting the people who are important to your partner is a significant step in a relationship. It signifies a deepening bond, a desire to weave your lives together, and a willingness to share your personal universe with someone special. But introducing a new partner to your inner circle, those friends and family who have witnessed your journey and shaped your world, can be a delicate dance. It requires sensitivity, a dash of cosmic awareness, and a thoughtful approach to interstellar integration.

First impressions matter, but they don't have to be a high-pressure performance. Instead of orchestrating a grand, formal introduction, consider starting with a casual encounter. Invite your partner to a low-key gathering where they can meet your friends or family members in a relaxed, informal setting. This allows for organic interactions, easing any potential awkwardness and giving everyone a chance to connect naturally.

Context is key when introducing your partner to your universe. Sharing anecdotes about your loved ones beforehand, their quirks, their passions, and their relationship to you, can help your partner navigate the social landscape with greater ease. It provides conversation starters, common ground, and a glimpse into the tapestry of relationships that have shaped your life.

Honoring your partner's comfort level is paramount. Not everyone is comfortable being thrust into the spotlight or engaging in deep conversations upon first meeting. Be mindful of their personality and social style, allowing them to acclimate to your world at their own pace.

Encourage your friends and family to do the same. Gentle encouragement to engage in conversation, to share stories, and to show genuine interest can go a long way in creating a welcoming and inclusive atmosphere.

Remember, introducing your partner to your loved ones is not a test or an audition. It's an opportunity for them to get to know each other, to discover shared interests, and to build connections organically.

Be prepared for a kaleidoscope of reactions. Your friends and family may express excitement, curiosity, or even a touch of reservation. These are all natural responses stemming from their love and concern for you. Be patient, answer their questions honestly, and reassure them that you value their opinions while also charting your own course in love.

Integration takes time. Don't expect your partner to seamlessly blend into your existing social dynamics overnight. Building relationships takes time, shared experiences, and a willingness to navigate the inevitable bumps along the way. Encourage your partner and your loved ones to spend time together in different settings, fostering connections through shared activities, conversations, and moments that celebrate the uniqueness of your expanded universe.

Ultimately, introducing your partner to your family and friends is about sharing your life with someone you care about. It's about creating a space where your loved ones can connect, share experiences, and hopefully, build relationships that enrich your life in countless ways. Embrace the journey, navigate the cosmos with an open heart, and remember that the most beautiful constellations are often formed when different worlds collide.

Keeping the Spark Alive Long Term Love in a Fast Paced Galaxy

Relationships, like stars, require constant energy to burn bright. In the whirlwind of a fast-paced life, maintaining that radiant glow of love and connection requires conscious effort, a sprinkle of stardust, and a commitment to nurturing the flame.

One of the most powerful ways to keep the spark alive is through the simple yet profound act of presence. In a world saturated with distractions, putting down your phone, silencing the notifications, and truly focusing on your partner speaks volumes. Listen attentively, not just to the words they speak, but to the unspoken emotions behind them. Offer eye contact that conveys genuine interest, a smile that speaks of shared joy, and a touch that reaffirms your connection.

Remember the power of small gestures. Grand romantic gestures have their place, but it's often the everyday acts of love and appreciation that sustain a relationship in the long run. A handwritten note tucked into a lunch bag, a spontaneous back rub after a long day, a shared cup of coffee on a busy morning – these seemingly small gestures create a constellation of connection that illuminates even the darkest of nights.

Shared experiences are the building blocks of lasting memories. In the tapestry of a relationship, it's not just about reaching the destination, but about savoring the journey together. Plan regular date nights, even if it's just a walk in the park or a movie night at home. Embrace new adventures, explore uncharted territories, and step outside your comfort zones together. Shared experiences, both big and small, infuse your relationship with a sense of adventure and keep the spark of discovery alive.

Growth, both individual and as a couple, is essential for long-term love to thrive. Just as stars evolve over time, so too do relationships. Encourage each other's passions, support personal growth, and celebrate each other's successes. Embrace the ebb and flow of life, knowing that change is inevitable and that navigating those changes together strengthens your bond.

Communication is the lifeblood of any relationship, but it's especially crucial in the long term. Create a safe space for open, honest dialogue, where you can express your needs, your fears, your dreams, and your desires without judgment. Listen with empathy, seeking to understand your partner's perspective, even when it differs from your own.

Remember that conflict is a natural part of any relationship. It's not about avoiding disagreements altogether, but about learning how to navigate them with respect, understanding, and a commitment to finding common ground.

Nurturing intimacy, both physical and emotional, is paramount. Physical touch, from holding hands to passionate embraces, releases oxytocin, the "cuddle hormone," which fosters feelings of closeness and connection. Emotional intimacy deepens when you share your inner world with your partner – your vulnerabilities, your fears, your hopes, and your dreams.

Finally, never underestimate the power of laughter. Life can be challenging, but shared laughter creates a sense of lightness, joy, and connection that can carry you through even the toughest of times. Find humor in the everyday moments, share inside jokes, and never lose sight of the joy and playfulness that drew you together in the first place.

Love, like a star, requires constant energy to burn bright. But with conscious effort, a sprinkle of stardust, and a commitment to nurturing the flame, your love story can illuminate the galaxy for a lifetime.

Chapter 6: The Search for Intelligent Life Finding Your Perfect Match Or at Least Someone Who Gets Your Jokes

Redefining The One Moving Beyond Fairytales and Embracing Realistic Expectations

"The One." It's a concept deeply woven into our cultural fabric, a shimmering thread running through countless fairytales, romantic comedies, and pop songs. We're raised on stories of destined lovers, two halves of a whole, finding their perfect match, their soulmate, their "one true love." But what happens when we carry these fairytale expectations into the real world of relationships?

The problem with clinging to the idealized notion of "The One" is that it sets us up for disappointment. It creates unrealistic expectations, blinding us to the beauty and potential of perfectly imperfect relationships. No one person can fulfill our every need, heal every wound, or align perfectly with every aspect of our being. We're all complex individuals, with our own unique histories, desires, and quirks.

Embracing realistic expectations begins with challenging the fairytale narrative. It's about recognizing that "The One" is not a preordained destiny, but rather a conscious choice to build a life with another human being, flaws and all. It's about understanding that relationships require effort, compromise, and a willingness to navigate the inevitable ups and downs that life throws our way.

Instead of searching for a mythical being who checks every box on an impossible list, shift your focus to finding someone who aligns with your values, shares your vision for the future, and inspires you to be the best version of yourself. Look for compatibility, not perfection. Seek a partner who challenges you to grow, who supports your dreams, and who accepts you, wholeheartedly, for the complex and ever-evolving being you are.

Remember that relationships are not about finding someone to complete you, but about choosing someone to share your journey with. It's about two individuals, each with their own unique strengths and weaknesses, coming together to create something beautiful and lasting.

Redefining "The One" also means embracing the ebb and flow of love. Passionate love, the kind that sets our souls on fire, is a powerful force, but it's not always a reliable indicator of long-term compatibility. Over time, that initial spark often transforms into a deeper, more enduring form of love – a love built on trust, respect, shared values, and a deep emotional connection.

Relationships require nurturing, just like a garden. It's about making a conscious effort to tend to the relationship, to water it with kindness, to fertilize it with shared experiences, and to prune away any negativity that threatens its growth.

Don't be afraid to seek support when needed. Just as we consult with experts in other areas of our lives, seeking guidance from a therapist or relationship counselor can provide valuable tools and insights to navigate challenges and strengthen your bond.

Ultimately, redefining "The One" is about embracing the beauty of imperfection, both in ourselves and in our partners. It's about letting go of fairytale expectations and choosing to build a love that is real, resilient, and deeply fulfilling. It's about recognizing that the most extraordinary love stories are often written not in grand gestures, but in the quiet moments of everyday connection, shared laughter, and unwavering support.

Trusting Your Intuition Recognizing the Signs of a True Cosmic Connection

Intuition – that whisper in your soul, that gut feeling, that inner knowing – is a powerful force, especially when it comes to matters of the heart. In a world saturated with external noise, learning to trust your intuition can be the compass that guides you towards a true cosmic connection.

A true cosmic connection often begins with a spark, an inexplicable pull towards another person. It's a feeling of resonance, as if your energies are harmonizing, creating a symphony of recognition. You might experience a sense of familiarity, as if you've known this person before, in another lifetime perhaps. Pay attention to those initial feelings, those subtle energetic exchanges. They often hold valuable clues about the potential of a connection.

One of the hallmarks of a true cosmic connection is a sense of ease, a feeling of coming home to yourself in the presence of another. Conversations flow effortlessly, silences are comfortable, and you feel seen, heard, and understood at a soul level. There's a natural alignment of values, beliefs, and life goals, creating a solid foundation for a relationship to flourish.

Trust your intuition when it speaks to you through synchronicities. These meaningful coincidences, often dismissed as mere chance, can be powerful signposts from the universe. Perhaps you keep running into this person in unexpected places, or you discover a shared love for a particular book, song, or hobby. These synchronicities are often the universe's way of nudging you towards a path of heart-centered connection.

Pay attention to how you feel when you're with this person. Does their presence uplift you, inspire you, and bring out the best version of yourself? Do you feel safe, supported, and cherished in their presence? Or do you find yourself questioning your worth, dimming your light, or compromising your values to fit in?

A true cosmic connection nourishes your soul. It feels expansive, empowering, and full of possibility. It inspires personal growth, encourages you to step into your authentic self, and supports you in pursuing your dreams.

Trust your intuition when it whispers words of caution. Just as it can guide you towards a true connection, it can also alert you to potential red flags. Pay attention to any inconsistencies between words and actions, any gut feelings that something isn't quite right. Don't dismiss those feelings or try to rationalize them away. Your intuition is your inner compass, guiding you towards what's truly best for you.

Remember that trusting your intuition is a process, not a destination. It takes time to develop a strong connection with your inner voice and to learn to discern its whispers from the cacophony of external noise. Practice mindfulness, meditation, or journaling to cultivate a deeper sense of self-awareness and to strengthen your intuition.

Trusting your intuition is not about abandoning logic or common sense. It's about finding a balance between the wisdom of your head and the wisdom of your heart. Gather information, assess the situation, but ultimately, trust that inner voice that speaks to you on a soul level.

Finding a true cosmic connection is a journey, not a destination. It's about embracing the unknown, trusting the timing of your life, and believing that the universe has a plan for you, even when you can't see the whole picture. Trust your intuition, listen to your heart, and allow yourself to be guided towards a love that is true, authentic, and deeply fulfilling.

Love in the Time of Chaos Building a Strong Foundation for a Lasting Relationship

Life is a whirlwind. It throws curveballs, presents unexpected detours, and sometimes feels like a chaotic dance across a tightrope. In the midst of this beautiful, messy chaos, building a strong foundation for a lasting relationship is like constructing a sanctuary – a haven where love can weather any storm.

The cornerstone of a strong foundation is open and honest communication. It's about creating a safe space where both partners feel seen, heard, and understood. Share your joys, your fears, your dreams, and your vulnerabilities with equal measure. Listen with empathy, seeking to understand your partner's perspective, even when it differs from your own. Remember, communication is not just about speaking your truth but also about truly listening, receiving, and understanding the other's heart.

Cultivate a shared vision for the future. What are your individual aspirations and how do they intertwine? Discuss your hopes, your dreams, and your long-term goals. When both partners are aligned on the bigger picture, it's easier to navigate the day-to-day challenges and to support each other's growth.

Embrace the power of compromise. No two individuals are identical, and differences are bound to arise. Instead of viewing disagreements as battles to be won, approach them as opportunities to find common ground. Be willing to bend, to meet in the middle, and to prioritize the health of the relationship over individual desires.

Nurture your emotional intimacy. Just as a garden requires regular watering, emotional intimacy needs consistent attention. Make time for deep conversations, share your innermost thoughts and feelings, and offer each other unwavering support. Celebrate each other's successes and provide comfort during times of need. Remember, emotional intimacy is the bedrock of a strong and resilient relationship.

Keep the flame of romance alive. Amidst the demands of daily life, it's easy for romance to fade into the background. Make a conscious effort to prioritize quality time together. Plan regular date nights, surprise each other with small gestures of affection, and never underestimate the power of a heartfelt compliment. Romance is the spark that ignites passion and keeps the love story exciting.

Weathering the storms of life requires resilience. Challenges are an inevitable part of any relationship, but it's how you face them together that determines your strength as a couple. Approach difficulties as a team, offering each other unwavering support and working together to find solutions. Remember, every storm has a silver lining, and navigating challenges together can deepen your bond and strengthen your foundation.

Never underestimate the power of forgiveness. We are all human, and mistakes are inevitable. Holding onto grudges or harboring resentment only creates distance and erodes the foundation of trust. Practice forgiveness, both for your partner and for yourself.

Let go of past hurts, extend grace, and focus on building a future filled with love and understanding.

Building a strong foundation for a lasting relationship is an ongoing process, a continuous dance between two individuals committed to creating something beautiful and enduring. It's about weathering the storms together, celebrating the joys, and nurturing the love that binds you. Embrace the chaos, for it's often in the midst of life's challenges that the strongest love stories are written.

Chapter 7: A Single Girls Guide to Galactic Domination: Embracing Singledom and Living Your Best Life

The Joys of Solo Travel Exploring the Universe on Your Own Terms

Solo travel. It's an invitation to embark on a journey of self-discovery, a passport to explore the world on your own terms, a symphony composed of freedom and flexibility. It's a chance to shed expectations, embrace spontaneity, and delve into the unknown with open arms and an adventurous spirit.

Imagine waking up in a foreign city, the day a blank canvas stretching before you. No need to consult itineraries, negotiate plans, or compromise on your desires. You are free to wander, to linger, to follow the whispers of your own curiosity. Perhaps you'll stumble upon a hidden café tucked away on a cobblestone street, or lose yourself in the vibrant energy of a local market. The beauty of solo travel lies in its unscripted nature, in the freedom to embrace the unexpected and to craft a journey that reflects the unique rhythm of your soul.

Traveling alone allows you to connect with your surroundings on a deeper level. Without the familiar comfort of a companion, your senses heighten, becoming more attuned to the sights, sounds, and scents of your environment. You'll find yourself engaging in conversations with locals, savoring the flavors of regional cuisine, and noticing the intricate details of ancient architecture with a newfound appreciation.

Solo travel is an opportunity to step outside of your comfort zone and embrace the unknown. It's a chance to challenge yourself, to test your limits, and to discover hidden reserves of strength and resilience you never knew you possessed. Whether it's navigating a foreign subway system, ordering a meal in another language, or simply finding the courage to strike up a conversation with a stranger, solo travel pushes you to grow in ways you never thought possible.

One of the most rewarding aspects of solo travel is the opportunity for profound self-reflection. As you wander through ancient ruins, hike through breathtaking landscapes, or simply relax on a sun-drenched beach, you'll find yourself with ample time for introspection. Without the distractions of daily life, you can delve into the depths of your own thoughts and feelings, gaining a deeper understanding of your values, your passions, and your place in the world.

Solo travel is also an invitation to connect with others in a meaningful way. Free from the confines of a pre-determined itinerary, you're more likely to engage in spontaneous conversations with fellow travelers and locals alike. You'll find yourself sharing stories, exchanging perspectives, and forging connections that transcend geographical boundaries.

Embrace the transformative power of solitude. In a world that constantly demands our attention, solo travel offers the gift of quiet contemplation. It's a chance to disconnect from the digital world, to silence the noise of everyday life, and to simply be present in the moment. Use this time for journaling, meditation, or simply allowing your thoughts to wander. You'll return home feeling refreshed, rejuvenated, and more connected to your inner self.

Remember, solo travel is not about being alone; it's about embracing the freedom to choose your own adventure. So, pack your bags, silence your doubts, and embark on a journey of self-discovery that will stay with you long after you return home. The world awaits, ready to reveal its secrets to those who dare to explore it on their own terms.

Cultivating Meaningful Connections The Importance of Friendships and Chosen Family

Human beings are wired for connection. We thrive in the presence of others, drawing strength, support, and inspiration from the tapestry of relationships that color our lives. While romantic love often takes center stage, it's crucial to remember the profound importance of friendships and chosen families in cultivating a life rich in meaning and connection.

Friendships are the heart and soul of our social landscape. They offer a safe haven to be ourselves, without pretense or judgment. True friends celebrate our joys, offer solace during times of sorrow, and challenge us to grow into the best versions of ourselves. They are the keepers of our secrets, the partners in crime on life's adventures, and the voices of reason when we stray from our paths.

Nurturing these precious bonds requires time, effort, and a generous spirit. Make time for coffee dates, phone calls, or simply sharing a quiet evening together. Listen with an open heart, offer support without judgment, and celebrate each other's milestones, both big and small. Remember, the language of friendship is spoken not just in words but also in shared laughter, heartfelt tears, and the unspoken understanding that comes from years of shared experiences.

In an increasingly interconnected world, the concept of chosen family has taken on profound significance. These are the friends who become more than just companions; they become the siblings we never had, the confidantes who know us better than we know ourselves, the people who show up for us, unconditionally, time and time again.

Chosen families are built on a foundation of shared values, mutual respect, and unwavering love. They are the people who embrace our quirks, accept our flaws, and love us through thick and thin. They are the ones we turn to for advice, for comfort, for a good laugh, and for a shoulder to cry on.

Building a chosen family is an act of intentional love. It's about surrounding ourselves with people who uplift us, inspire us, and make us feel seen and valued for who we truly are. It's about creating a circle of support that transcends blood ties and societal expectations, a space where we can be our authentic selves, without apology or reservation.

The beauty of chosen families lies in their diversity. They can encompass people from all walks of life, from different cultures, backgrounds, and age groups. This richness of experience adds depth and dimension to our lives, challenging our perspectives, broadening our horizons, and reminding us that love knows no bounds.

In a world that can often feel isolating, cultivating meaningful connections is essential for our emotional well-being. Friendships and chosen families provide a sense of belonging, a reminder that we are not alone in navigating the complexities of life. They offer a safety net of support, a source of strength during challenging times, and a constant wellspring of joy and laughter.

So, cherish your friends, nurture your chosen family, and invest in the relationships that make your heart sing. For it is in the warmth of human connection that we truly come alive, finding solace, meaning, and an enduring sense of belonging.

Falling in Love with Yourself Prioritizing Self Care Self Discovery and Personal Growth

Falling in love with yourself. It's not about vanity or ego, but a deep and abiding appreciation for the incredible, complex, and beautiful being that you are. It's about embracing your strengths, acknowledging your vulnerabilities, and committing to a lifelong journey of self-discovery and personal growth.

Self-care is the foundation upon which self-love is built. It's not a luxury, but a necessity, a non-negotiable aspect of living a fulfilling and meaningful life. It's about tuning into your physical, emotional, and mental needs and honoring them with intention and care.

Start by nourishing your body with wholesome foods, regular exercise, and adequate rest. These are not just tasks to check off a list, but acts of self-respect, a way of honoring the vessel that carries you through life. Move your body in ways that bring you joy, whether it's dancing, hiking, swimming, or simply stretching under the morning sun.

Just as you nourish your body, it's essential to feed your soul. Engage in activities that spark your creativity, ignite your passions, and bring you a sense of peace and fulfillment. Lose yourself in a good book, explore a new hobby, spend time in nature, or surround yourself with beauty in its many forms.

Self-discovery is an integral part of the journey towards self-love. It's about peeling back the layers, silencing the inner critic, and embracing the unique tapestry of your being. Explore your values, your beliefs, your passions, and your dreams. What makes your heart sing? What are you deeply curious about? What legacy do you want to leave behind?

Embrace the transformative power of introspection. Carve out time for quiet reflection, whether it's through journaling, meditation, or simply spending time in nature. Listen to the whispers of your heart, pay attention to your dreams, and allow yourself the space to explore the depths of your own being.

Personal growth is not about striving for perfection, but about embracing the journey of becoming the best version of yourself. It's about identifying areas where you want to grow, setting intentions, and taking small, consistent steps towards your goals.

Embrace challenges as opportunities for learning and growth. Step outside of your comfort zone, embrace new experiences, and don't be afraid to fail. It's through our failures that we often learn the most valuable lessons, gaining resilience, wisdom, and a deeper understanding of ourselves.

Surround yourself with people who support your journey, who uplift you, inspire you, and challenge you to grow. Seek out mentors, connect with like-minded individuals, and create a circle of support that encourages you to blossom into the best version of yourself.

Remember, falling in love with yourself is not a destination, but a lifelong adventure. It's a journey filled with peaks and valleys, moments of joy and times of challenge. Embrace it all, for it is in the totality of your experiences that you will discover the depth of your own strength, the beauty of your own spirit, and the boundless capacity of your own heart.